Lehi Runs Away

written by Tiffany Thomas
illustrated by Nikki Casassa

CFI • An imprint of Cedar Fort, Inc. • Springville, Utah

HARD WORDS:
city, family, follow

PARENT TIP: Choose one or two words for the child to read, with you reading the more difficult words. Each time you read through the story, have them read an additional one or two new words.

This is Lehi.

Lehi is a
man of God.

The city is bad.

Lehi prays
to God.

God says
to run away.

Lehi and his family run away.

Lehi lives in a tent.

God gives Lehi a ball.

The ball says where to go.

Lehi and his sons
follow the ball.

Lehi sees the sea.

The end.

ISBN 13: 978-1-4621-4337-5

Published by CFI, an imprint of Cedar Fort, Inc. • 2373 W. 700 S., Suite 100, Springville, UT 84663
Distributed by Cedar Fort, Inc., www.cedarfort.com

Cover design and interior layout design by Shawnda T. Craig
Cover design © 2022 Cedar Fort, Inc.
Printed in China • Printed on acid-free paper
10 9 8 7 6 5 4 3 2 1